Mirrors, Myths, and Dreams

poems by

Malcolm Glass

Finishing Line Press
Georgetown, Kentucky

Mirrors, Myths, and Dreams

ACKNOWLEDGMENTS

"On the Summit of Mount Abraham" was published in *High Plains Register.*

Publisher: Leah Maines
Editor: Christen Kincaid
Cover Art: Jane R. Glass
Author Photo: Malcolm Glass
Cover Design: Elizabeth Maines McCleavy

Printed in the USA on acid-free paper.
Order online: www.finishinglinepress.com
          also available on amazon.com

Author inquiries and mail orders:
Finishing Line Press
P. O. Box 1626
Georgetown, Kentucky 40324
U. S. A.

Table of Contents

Mirrors I

Love Child

A woman in a pleated skirt,
dull brown shoes, and a blouse
loose around her shoulders,
carried her baby from the hospital
in a woven basket, blankets tucked
around her face, to protect her
from the cold, the rain, the tears
she never saw. The windy chill
of a North Carolina autumn
swirled around them as they drove
south in a 1944 DeSoto. The willow
basket creaked as they rounded
the curves and stopped for red lights
in Georgia. Their journey moved
into darkness and emerged
in the gray light of another dawn.

In Jacksonville, beyond heavy
doors, a nurse took the child
to the nursery where bottle
after bottle would sustain her
through three months of waiting
for the strangers who would be
her parents. A bracelet held
a number close to the delicate
pulse in her wrist, the blood
carrying the code of her identity,
those strands twisting through
the silent decades, but returning,
always, to this November day.

Fevered

My head buried under thick
terry cloth, I breathed in
the bite of Mentholatum steam.
In the light suffused by the towel
across the back of my head,
islands of quivering oil
drifted in the hot water.
I sat on a stool, hunched
over the basin, my face hot
in camphor mist, wheezing
a loosened rattle in my chest.

On my shoulders my mother's
hands rested, almost weightless,
and then they began their careful
ritual, kneading my fevered
muscles, her thumbs working
down between my shoulder
blades, as if searching
for hidden buds of wings.

Leaves

Early in October I swam home
through the dense air of Florida,
holding steady at eighty-seven
degrees in the late afternoon sun.
In my first grade writing tablet I carried
brittle leaves—maple, oak, and poplar—
leaves I had cut from paper and colored
orange, yellow, red, following carefully
the teacher's directions, leaves I had
never seen on the trees or ground
of Florida. She had written *Autumn*
across the blackboard—foreign letters,
a distant sound. I knew I had to learn
such things. How could I grow up
without knowing about pygmies
or polar bears? How could I be
smart without penguins, tumbleweeds,
the rivers India? But I already
knew leaves, and pine needles,
all about me, either green on the tree,
or brown on the ground. Nothing
in between, no slow, colorful dying.

My autumn leaves stayed for weeks,
scattered down the arctic glacier
of the refrigerator door. Finally
I piled them on the top shelf
of my closet. Forgotten, vanished.
Like so much I think I know.

Birthday Friends

My sixth birthday, slipping
through the mirror of memory,
leaves me a blur of questions:
Was that the day Cissy Wilson
chased me through the Boston
ferns? The day I asked Lena Anne
Sawyer to marry me? The first
time Mummy spread thick peanut
butter frosting on a chocolate
cake made from scratch?

I find no answers in this photo,
dog-eared, gone thin brown.
We squint against the Florida
glare, the burnt grass crackling
at our Buster Browns, first graders
arranged in the traditional
ceremony of remembrance.

My mother held the Kodak
Brownie box camera steady
against her waist, shielding
the viewfinder with her hand
and staring down into that tiny
window at our faces, mere specks,
our smiles and frowns, invisible.

On the back of the snapshot,
she wrote every name. I don't recall
Ann or Lucy, and Bruce is only
a face in the doorway of his home
by the lake. Some of these friends

stayed with me from first through
twelfth grade and then disappeared.
My mother would be the first
to tell me if any of these children
had died. If she were still here.

Eugene's Cards

Aunt Ethel kept her playing cards
in an old sewing basket behind
the davenport for when we came
to visit. After supper she gathered
my sisters Linda, Polly, and me
around her rickety card table
for Snip snap snorem. "Love
one another," she'd say.
"No spats and no cussing."

One night I said, "Let's use
the cards with the bicycles."
"No, honey, them's Eugene's."
Gene was her only son, her only
child. He drowned in the quarry
his senior year. "He done his magic
with them cards. They's sacred.
Never been touched by nobody else."
Ethel started to cry and covered
her mouth with a napkin. "I'm sorry,
Auntie," I said. "It's all right,
son. You didn't mean nothing by it."
She patted my hand. "Sometimes
it catches me by surprise is all.
Whose turn is it? Come on, boy,
you're going to win this hand."

Lost Child

My mother turns the page, like pulling back
a veil, revealing your face in the album.
Dusty brown, fading and pale against
black, you stare out at us, smiling
cautiously, as though you weren't sure
a smile was proper. Grandma says,
"He looks like you, Carl." "Not me,"
I say. "I'd never wear a shirt like that."

Distant cousin, stranger, you are no one
to us, though we know you should be.
Perhaps you are now a plumber
in Peoria or an accountant in Nutley,
New Jersey. You may have died
in your twenties of a heart defect
waiting patiently in your chest
to take you from us. "I think that

may be Buster Lisenbee," says Uncle
Milton. "You know, cousin Bill's
cousin who made it big in the minor
leagues." "I think you're right," I say.
"He was a star at Westhaven High."
And we bring you back into the fold, safe
from an untimely death and the purgatory
of nameless and forgotten souls.

Don

In a small snapshot I am standing
under the tall long-needle pines,
between my white terrier Skipper
and Don, Bishop John D. Wing's
handsome German shepherd.
Behind us the lawn of Bishopstead
sprawls to the shore of Lake Osceola.

We stayed at the Wing's elegant home
in the summers, to keep the windows
open, to defeat mildew, mold,
and clotted salt. And to care for Don.

Every evening, Dad, Skipper, Don,
and I walked down Interlachen Avenue,
lined with lake-side estates, vast
lawns and landscaping rich
with primal scents threaded under
the ligustrum and along the roots
of broad-limbed water oaks.
Don and Skipper tracked the trails
of raccoon, rabbit, and squirrel,
panting with glee as they ran.

Don loved hunting the living and quick,
running squirrels up trees, barking
at their hostile chatter. His favorite
prey was our cat Pixie until she had
had enough of that and pounced
on his back, dug in, and rode him
as he yelped and spun in manic circles.

Whenever my father took his rowboat
trolling for perch, Don would wait
on the dock for his return. At the end
of one summer my father rowed
to the far side of the lake to chain
his boat to the cypress where he kept it
the rest of the year, and then he walked
to our house on Lasbury Avenue
to spend the night. The next morning,
when Dad drove back to Bishopstead,
he found Don waiting for him
on the dock, asleep in the early sunlight.

That year, after the Wings returned
from their cool respite in Vermont,
the note card from Don, in the Bishop's
scrawly, doggy handwriting, arrived,
thanking me for taking care of him,
for being his buddy, along with Skipper,
on our evening walks, and for keeping
his bowls filled with water and Alpo.

I kept it for years in a box of letters
my mother sent me in college. I can't
find it now. But I do have this tattered,
fading photograph, taken one summer,
perhaps our last together: the dogs
on either side of me, Skipper, bristly
white, standing at attention, and Don,
his head bowed, his shoulders hunched,
so much older than I remembered.

Queenie

Note: A new process of freeze-drying now makes it possible to preserve pets in a state more life-like than taxidermy.

On the braided rug before the hearth
lies Queenie, the envy of Pharaohs,
her head turned, so, alert, staring
up at me, at anyone who sits here,
at the tan water stain on the ceiling
when the chair is empty. I turn to Janet,
Queenie's mistress, very much alive,
and wonder at technology, the miracles
quick and bitter cold perform. I see,
with Janet's guidance, how lustrously
Queenie's coat glistens in the gas-log
firelight, and take her word the vacuum
cleaner bag has never been so free
of Queenie's wiry hair.

Through our discourse, Queenie
lies still, heedless of the coming
and going of seasons beyond
the window: leaves twist forth, spin
to the ground, emerge tightly again,
months later. While the wind shifts
between the poles—balmy, frigid,
sultry—Queenie's skin steadies
between seventy and seventy-five
degrees, basking in the air-conditioned
chill, temperate in her winter coat.

For all I know, her dreams and memories
may still be with her, locked in frozen
brain cells: clouds shading chipmunk
burrows, the threads of scent squirrels
drag through heaps of fallen leaves.

Janet smiles and says, again, "Everything
about Queenie is the same." Bruno,
the miniature dachshund, Queenie's
lifelong fellow traveler those long
walks in the park, cringes in the doorway,
whimpering. "Isn't that sweet?"
Janet says. "Even Bruno remembers."

Beauregard Tiberius

Beauregard Tiberius, docile
gray Persian, my sister's beloved,
my eight years did not match
your eight, your fifty-six years
of feline composure and wisdom.

One afternoon, out of boredom,
I pulled out the Electrolux
to vacuum the living room carpet.
The buzzing whine drove you
under the maroon wingback,
over the ottoman, and behind
the sofa. With the wand and brush
I chased your fluttering plume
tail as you climbed the draperies.

Fifty-six of my years later,
my gray Persian Jefferson
basks in my care, my attention
to his bowl, brush, and box.
His whispered snores flutter
across the crazy quilt. At my touch
he purrs, as he stretches from sleep.

And I think of you, Beau, as I did
not then, of your heart set loose
in your chest with feverish
palpitation, of the sudden burn
of adrenalin through your veins,
your muscles driving you in panic
from the evil wail of the vacuum
pulling at your breath.

Beauregard, it is not only Jeffy
I love now, as memory falls
through the years, reaching back
to the forgiveness only an animal
could give so purely. You call to me
still from the powder of your bones.

Minnaloushe's Dream

—for W. B. Yeats and Iseult Gonne

In the house of tall doors, seaweed drifts
into the skylight of broken mice,
and starry, stubborn waves of dust lift

a chorus of scratch marks, like brown rice
tossed against bright windowpanes in rooms
filled with the stiff aroma of spiced

rum.   Minnaloushe's silver tail brooms
the scattered confetti of the sky,
into golden twig and carmine bloom,

tumbling them in a gather of dry
lightning. From the shaken driftweed sea
orange daylily petals fall and fly

into tufted flocks of glade-loud bees
swarming over a marmalade tree.

Myths and Dreams

The Dryad Erato

My eyes enfold your secret
dream of skin grazing muscle
tendon bone, the quick pulse

of a cloudless blush to thaw
your veins. I offer you my still,
wordless lips, promising

evermore bristling shivers.
Here is the piquant taste
of my nibble-kiss, to quicken

your stuttering heartbeat.
Take the honeyed swirl
of my tongue to sweeten

your mouth, my barkbite
to spark your coiled hair.

Dream of the Maenad Hedone

The thin shadows of dawn

clouds flicker across her lips,
her eyelids, her blue-veined

throat. Echoes of the driven
pulse of drums beat at the heart
of her dream: her sisters

churning sod and blade.
Fevered incantations, lips
burgundied, the frantic
shake of terracotta curls,

Fingers knitted, tight, tender,
the copper burnish of firelight
on shin and wrist, on sweat
and flex of tendon, joint,

and thigh. As the scrim
of night falls, her eyes stutter
open, to ghosts, to wisps of smoke

escaping the bonfire embers
to rise and breathe again

in the thickening clouds.

The Naiad Muriel

Stones float below me,
pale clouds shadowing
the meadows. Feathers

of long grass lift the wind
over my feet. I hold a birch
branch for the final coming

of crow. His sheen echoes
midnight, and his vibrant
cries urge my quiet brook

toward the jade sea. Crow
rises, spiraling into the eye
of the new moon, his indigo

words breaking open the shell
of the dream beyond dawn.

Cassandra, Kyprian Sibyl of the Hart

A gust of dry wind, like the ghost
of the hunt, leans the dried grasses
westward, singing the forgotten

heartbeats of the hounds, the hunters,
the noble hart. Field and hillside
shake with jewels of blood,

the nodding heads of poppies.
I hold my talisman, this skull
whose teeth, when sown

in the clouds, bring down rain
and a prayer for all things falling
to stillness. My mudra holds

a calm spiral of Maya blue light
in the twisting whirlwind of mist.

Ania's Song
—the Greek goddess of sorrow

At the monument I kneel
before the frieze carved
in gray stone immemorial:

the bodies of the fallen: my lover,
his comrades in blood, the loyal
horses. With my hands I cover

my eyes to stop the tears,
but they fall, my song for him,
for all of them, for all of us.

The line of my threnody rises,
wavering. It stretches in longing
toward the stars. What is my hope

now? I have only the rich harmonies
entwining this melody I weep
to stay me until I join him.

Haunted

On the cold riverbank, tangled
with fallen branches, lies
a porcelain doll, swaddled

in a child's overcoat, its feet
caught under a limb, an arm
clogged in mud, and one

eye, violet blue, frozen
open. The story the doll
knows but cannot tell:

flames whipping worn
linen curtains against
a broken window.

Beyond the panes, winter grass,
and snow gathering still.

Moonbreak

In the core of my night,
my feet blind, I stumbled,
seeking in the mud a buried

pathway, with roots and vines
dragging me down into
a darkened heartbeat, a web

of words thick on my tongue.
Moonbreak in a clearing
struck me down by a silver

pond.   My face rose before me,
halos of moons in my eyes,
and beyond the mirror

of water, a cascade of hills
echoing the blue clouds.

Mirrors II

Windshield

Clots of clouds drift across the panes,
rain-spattered, streaked rusty pink,
like blood-mist sinking into the chalices
of maroon tulips busted through April
in a charmed ring circling the bird bath
dead center in the yard of a double-wide.

A barking truck horn scatters vultures
in a squall-gust of wings, as they flee
the deer carcass behind the Church
of the Eternal Rock of Jesus and God's
Holy Tongues. The signboard leans
roadward, plastic letters in the ditch.

The mumbling creek behind Barton's
rattle-board barn runs thick and clear
under the swinging bridge, rope-slung
bank to bank, the only way to the house,
to the white siding splotched with algae.
Out back a Plymouth hunkers down.

A sprawl of wet magazines clogs
the drainage ditch. Windows blackened
with soot watch for the next rain storm.
On the rusting floorboard, patched
with duct tape, a powder-blue blouse,
a garnet bracelet, a lipsticked cigarette.

The windshield, glazed dull pearl,
still shelters cracked visors, a dead
odometer, a frozen gearshift lever,
the ghost of a hand learning the stretch
of nylon, the slide of silk skin,
the petaled grail rich with dew.

Across the Bed
            —after Arthur Miller

The rails of the el slice close
to the neon sign: Hotel Arkansas.
Stuttering wheels of the swaying
wooden cars drum a syncopated
rumble, and shake the window
in its fragile casement, raining oily
soot on the chipped paint of the sill.

Above the iron bed, tilting
warily, hangs a pallid picture
of two children fishing beside
a mill wheel.   On the small oak
dresser a leather suitcase yawns
at the ceiling. The steady chatter
of water filling the bathtub sings
an ostinato to Crosby's warbling
descant. Then a tired hand turns
off the radio, and a woman's voice
wavers faintly, "Don't tell me
that you know the ending."

A pair of copper brown wingtips,
cross-hatched with scars, sits
hidden from view under the bed.
In the suitcase a crumpled white
shirt with gritty collar and cuffs
hides under an olive green wool
suit, a twisted challis necktie,
and a navy blue handkerchief
embroidered with a maroon L.

Spread lovingly across the bed,
a pair of gauzy white silk stockings.

Weekend Landscapes

One wall of their motel room
was thick with lichens, sea-foam
green and rust, spreading down
the trunks of fallen trees. Across
the forest floor lay a sprawl
of jade moss and clusters of ferns.
In the far distance, a stand of pines
and firs drowned in the undertow
of noon sun. The bed seemed
to float at the edge of the landscape,
a photo blown to mural, grainy, cold.

During that winter weekend
they had waited twenty years for,
she stared over his thin shoulder
at the ivory sky, mottled with tan
stains from the leaky roof,
clouds unmoving, hard-edged.

In the thin light leaking around
the bathroom door, she hovered
above him, staring over the low
headboard at the dim forest
of decaying timber, the world
held in a sea of frozen pixels,
like a pointilistic painting.

Through a snowy morning beyond
the draperies, she sought camels,
ships, or elephants in the rainless
clouds above her, but no visions
or memories emerged in that sky
to carry her into a landscape rich
with vibrant breathing and tears.

Weeks later, she got the post card
he had found in the desk drawer,
a collage: the pool, the lounge,
another room with trees climbing
a mountainside above the TV screen.
And she felt, again, her shoulder
blades pressed into the bristling
ferns, vines binding her feet, lichens
scraping her back, as he moved her
insistently into the landscape.

On the Summit of Mt. Abraham

Moss and lichen listen to the wind.
We kiss. Kiss again, filling the silence
with silence. My fingers, pungent
with pine pitch, I caress your cheek,
flushed after our climb. Shadows
deepen along the hem of your shorts,
and my pulse sings in my eardrums.

Last summer we loved on the beach
in sheer, relentless light. I drowned
in your shadowless eyes, swam
in the heat nagging at your skin,
the sand peppering your collarbone,
the flare across hip and breast.
In the dunes we climbed the sunlight
breaking the waves, and fell,
fevered and delirious with feasting.

We sit now on boulders among stunted
pines, the canopy of firs pulling noon
darkness around our shoulders.
You hug your knees, shiver, and lean
against me. Pulling an apple
from your pack, you bite in
with a sharp crack, releasing the sly
music of its scent. My fingers enter
the shadow falling across your thigh
and find the hidden secret of taut elastic
and damp tendrils clinging to cool skin.

On your shoulder, ribs, and hip
bone I mingle traces of pine scent
with the fading perfume of apples.
We kiss. I bite into the other side
of your apple, throw the core
into the wind, and we begin again
the climb, the ascent beyond geography.

Lost Lake Found

I followed the railroad
tracks frazzled with tall
grass. The bend beyond

the tunnel knew how far
to lean me, and late summer
butterflies swirled me through

a copse to a field heavy-
laden with goldenrod, spilling
down to the curve of shore

and a plain—blue, marbled
by wind. Shimmering gold
foil flakes hovered above

the water, a host of dragonflies
whose lake was never lost.

Asian Lady Beetles

They do fly, these little buttons,
orange and yellow, spotted
black. One of them leapt
from a hawthorn leaf
and landed on my forehead
to give me a quick bite
hello, then spun away
on invisible
wings.

But most of the time I see them
crawling across the furry
leaf of an African violet
on the sill, or tracking the edge
of the stainless steel
sink.

I rescue these good luck omens
when they wander and fall
into stacked plates
and cups filled with water
deep enough for
drowning.

A beetle opens her shell
and spreads her wings
when she knows
it is time to die.
She holds very still, head
bowed as though in
prayer.

Beyond dying, she will fly
heavenward to nip
an angel hello
and to crawl across shiny
plains and dusky
jade hills
forever.

Revising the Past

I sit in the living room with my son Brian
and his friends, on couches facing each other.
We are making sure my son is not left alone
in his grieving. We stare at the recent past
held in a broken mirror, splinters of silver
scattered before us on the maroon carpet.
We pick up shards and fragments and try
to rub away the images we see there
so that when we put the mirror together
again on the wall of Lynn's bedroom,
it will show the carpet and dresser, the lamp
and curtains as they were the day before.

Brian's roommate Ricky rubs his shirt
sleeve on the reflection of the photograph
of Lynn's father in its broken frame.
With my handkerchief I try to wipe away
Lynn's fingerprints from the handle
of the pistol. At our feet lie slivered
images waiting for us to clean: spattered
wallpaper, the curtains Lynn's mother
tore from their rods, the dark stain
on the carpet seeping down to find
the blood her father left a year ago.

Dogwoods

—for Hibbard Thatcher
"Farewell, friend, earthly
light become heavenly."

The dogwoods bow
as wind blusters through
their leaves and sleeping buds.

They lean in a waltz,
limbs crossing allemande
left, nodding circles dos-a-dos
and promenades into the hollows.

The dogwoods bend
and genuflect, tossing coins
of sunlight and flags of shadows
across the earth, like the consonants
of plucked strings, the vowels and syllables

of praise. In their dance
and hymning, the dogwoods
mirror light rising through nebulae,
wheeling toward the first breath of the stars.

Malcolm Glass has published poetry, fiction, and non-fiction widely for sixty years. His work has appeared in many journals, including *Poetry* (Chicago), *Nimrod, The Laurel Review, The Sewanee Review,* and *Prairie Schooner.* Heinemann published his guide to writing poetry, *Important Words* (with Bill Brown); and he is the author of a half dozen books published by Scholastic Books. His books of poetry include *Bone Love, In the Shadow of the Gourd, The Dinky Line,* and *Malcolm Glass: Greatest Hits.*

A number of his poems have been set to music by contemporary composers, including Jack Williams's "Four Glass Poems" for orchestra, chorus and soloists; and his play "Sisters" was given a reading at La Mama Playhouse in New York. Glass has given poetry readings at the Universities of Florida, Michigan, New Hampshire, and many others.

Also an art photographer, his work has been shown in galleries and exhibitions from New York to Los Angeles. He has won many awards in juried exhibitions in the southeast, from Honorable Mention to Best of Show.

Glass co-directed the Creative Writing Program at Austin Peay State University, and for many years served as an editor of *The Cumberland Poetry Review* and as co-editor of *Zone 3 Literary Journal.*

He is a Fulbright Scholar, and a recipient of Stetson University's Distinguished Alumni Award. At Austin Peay State University he was awarded the Distinguished Professor Award and the Richard M. Hawkins Award for Creative Achievement.

As a writer Glass has been guided by a comment W. H. Auden made to him fifty-seven years ago: 'The best way to become a good poet is to write oneself through the history of poetry in English.' His mentors are the poems of Browning, Yeats, Thomas, Frost, Auden, Nemerov, and Wilbur.

www.ingramcontent.com/pod-product-compliance
Lightning Source LLC
LaVergne TN
LVHW051609080426
835510LV00020B/3197